DC
COMICS™

SUPERMAN
SCIENCE

SOARING THE SKIES

SUPERMAN™ AND THE SCIENCE OF FLIGHT

BY *TAMMY ENZ*

SUPERMAN CREATED BY
JERRY SIEGEL
AND **JOE SHUSTER**
BY SPECIAL ARRANGEMENT
WITH THE JERRY SIEGEL FAMILY

T0052459

CAPSTONE PRESS
a capstone imprint

Published by Capstone Press in 2016
A Capstone Imprint
1710 Roe Crest Drive
North Mankato, Minnesota 56003
www.mycapstone.com

STAR36204

Library of Congress Cataloging-in-Publication Data
Names: Enz, Tammy, author.
Title: Soaring the skies : Superman and the science of flight / by Tammy Enz.
Description: North Mankato, Minnesota : Capstone Press, 2016. | 2016 | Series: DC super
  heroes. Superman science | Audience: Ages 9–12. | Audience: Grade 3 to grade 6. |
  Includes bibliographical references and index.
Identifiers: LCCN 2016002666| ISBN 9781515709138 (library binding) | ISBN 9781515709176
  (paperback) | ISBN 9781515709213 (ebook pdf)
Subjects: LCSH: Flight—Juvenile literature. | Aerodynamics—Juvenile literature. |
  Superman (Fictitious character)—Juvenile literature.
Classification: LCC TL547 .E59 2016 | DDC 629.132—dc23
LC record available at http://lccn.loc.gov/2016002666

Summary: Explores the real-world science and engineering related to Superman's ability
to fly.

Editorial Credits
Editor: Christopher Harbo
Designer: Bob Lentz
Production Specialist: Tori Abraham
Media Researcher: Eric Gohl

Photo Credits
DVIDS: Staff Sgt. Jonathan Snyder, 26 (bottom); iStockphoto: Joe_Potato, 9 (top), Vasily
Smirnov, 28; Library of Congress: 8, 10 (all); NASA: 29, Tony Landis, 25 (top); National
Archives and Records Administration: 11; Shutterstock: Al Mueller, 19 (bottom), Aleksei
Lazukov, 13 (top), Alexandra Lande, 12, Andrey Khachatryan, 25 (bottom), Attila Jandi, 18,
Betto Rodrigues, 15, Boykov, 23 (bottom), Christian Mueller, 9 (bottom), Daniel Huebner,
16, eddtoro, 14, Ensuper, cover, FloridaStock, 7 (bottom), Jari Sokka, 20 (top), Lee Yiu Tung,
17 (right), Lu Yao, 27, Mariia Tagirova, 21, muratart, 7 (top), OPIS Zagreb, 24, Peter Vrabel,
20 (bottom), Ryan M. Bolton, 17 (bottom left), Sindre T, 13 (bottom), Tony Campbell, 17 (top
left), Werner Lehmann, 19 (top); USAF: 23 (top), TSgt. Effrain Lopez, 26 (top), TSgt. Michael
Haggerty, 22

Printed in the United States of America.
010491R

TABLE OF CONTENTS

UP, UP, AND AWAY!

With an effortless leap, Superman bounds into the air. No wings. No engines. No special gear or gadgets. Just a cape and his unique ability to defy the scientific laws that keep us grounded. Imagine what it would be like to have his power of flight. Where would you go? What would you see?

For thousands of years, flight really was something people could only dream about. But these days, soaring the skies is not limited to super heroes. While we lack the Man of Steel's superpowers, the ability to fly is well within our grasp. In fact, we often take it for granted. Almost anywhere on this planet is just a plane ride away.

But have you ever stopped to think about what makes flight possible? For instance, how does a hang glider stay aloft with no engine to power it? Or what helps a massive jumbo jet get off the ground? The answers are simple—science, engineering, and a little inspiration from nature. From wingsuits and fighter jets to flying fish and stealth aircraft, get ready to explore the incredible world of flight.

FACT:

When Superman first appeared in comics in 1938, he could leap great distances and over tall buildings. It wasn't until the early 1940s that he was shown to actually fly.

FLIGHT LESSONS

One second Clark Kent peels off his shirt and tie. The next, Superman soars over Metropolis. Flight is child's play for Superman, but it challenged scientists and engineers for centuries. Now their discoveries in flight science allow us to touch the clouds.

THE PHYSICS OF FLIGHT

Flight takes many forms. Birds flap their wings and airplanes use jet engines. But both must deal with gravity. Gravity is the force that pulls all objects toward Earth. Everything dropped, launched, or flown falls to Earth unless it overcomes gravity. To do that, fliers must employ **thrust** to move them forward through the air. Aircraft get thrust from their powerful engines. Birds experience thrust when they flap their wings.

But forward thrust alone won't keep fliers airborne. They must also create **lift**, or an upward force, to overcome gravity. Birds and planes have shaped wings to help create lift, but they only work when moving. An airplane doesn't create lift if its engines fail to push it forward. And while birds can glide without flapping, gravity pulls them down as their thrust decreases.

Commercial jets use powerful engines and shaped wings to achieve the thrust and lift necessary for liftoff.

LOW ENERGY LIFT

Eagles and other birds of prey are experts at creating lift with little effort. Their heavy bodies make flapping tiresome. Instead, these birds seek out thermal currents. Without flapping, they ride rising pockets of warm air upward for hundreds of feet.

thrust—the force that pushes a vehicle forward

lift—the upward force of air that causes an object to fly

thermal—having to do with heat or holding in heat

AERODYNAMIC AIRFOIL

Does Superman's cape hold the secret to his flight powers? No. But the way it cuts through the air might just give the Man of Steel a little extra lift. In the real world, the shape of an airplane's wings is the key to staying airborne.

Otto Lilienthal with one of his gliders in 1895.

The design of the modern airplane wing dates back more than 120 years. In the 1890s, bird wings inspired German engineer Otto Lilienthal to experiment with **airfoils**. An airfoil is a gently curved blade shape that causes air to move quicker over its top than its bottom. This movement creates lower air pressure above the wing to suck it upward. Meanwhile, the angle of the wing redirects air downward. As air is pushed down, the wing experiences lift as it is pushed up.

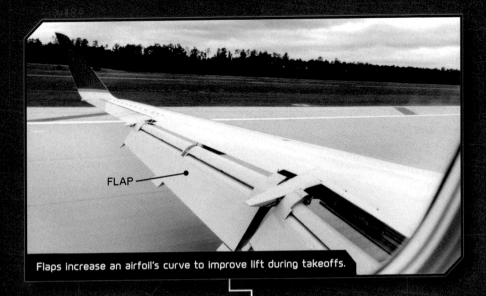

FLAP

Flaps increase an airfoil's curve to improve lift during takeoffs.

Staying aloft is one thing, but how does an airfoil help a heavy passenger jet take off? At takeoff, pilots lower flaps on the back of a jet's wings. These flaps make the airfoil's curve larger to increase lift. At 160 to 180 miles (258 to 290 kilometers) per hour, enough lift is created to raise the jet. While flying, the flaps are retracted to reduce **air resistance**, or drag. The reduced drag helps the plane cruise at 550 to 580 miles (885 to 933 km) per hour.

STOPPING POWER

Aircraft wings are shaped to reduce drag, but they also have features to increase it. Why? Because stopping a loaded plane landing at 150 miles (240 km) per hour is no small feat. Jets need more than their brakes to stop. They also use spoilers. These wing flaps flip up to create more drag to help stop the plane.

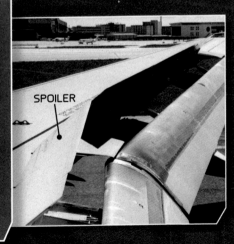

SPOILER

airfoil—a curved surface causing lift in flight

air resistance—the force of air rubbing against things

HUMAN HIGH-FLIERS

Superman is a symbol of our desire to be better, stronger, and faster. Likewise, his ability to soar the skies is a reminder of our long-held fascination with flight. And that fascination has led to some pretty amazing contraptions.

FOUNDERS OF FLIGHT

Dreams of human flight date back hundreds of years. In the 1400s, Leonardo DaVinci created more than 100 drawings that showed his ideas for flying machines. But it wasn't until the 1890s that human flight really took off. Otto Lilienthal's attempts to fly the first gliders inspired the scientists and engineers who eventually shaped the future of flight.

Two of those people were Orville and Wilbur Wright. Building on Lilienthal's ideas, the Wright brothers ushered in the era of powered flight. On December 17, 1903, their plane lifted off in Kitty Hawk, North Carolina. It stayed aloft for just 12 seconds and only covered about 120 feet (37 meters). But that short hop changed flight forever.

Orville Wright

Wilbur Wright

Orville Wright flies one of his early planes at Fort Myer, Virginia, in September 1908.

In a few short years, flight innovation skyrocketed. In 1914, planes were used in World War I (1914–1918) spy missions. By the end of the war they were being used for bombing runs and air combat. Not long after, overseas flight became a reality. On June 14, 1919, John Alcock and Arthur Brown made the first nonstop flight across the Atlantic. It took them 16 hours in a modified British Vimy bomber.

THE FIRST HELICOPTER

Igor Sikorsky developed the rotor designs for the first successful mass-produced helicopter. His skeletal VS-300 took flight on September 14, 1939. It made helicopter history by staying airborne for only a few seconds. But modern helicopters still use Sikorsky's main rotor and tail rotor design today.

UNPOWERED FLIGHT

The Man of Steel flies completely unassisted. He punches through the clouds without jet engines or rocket boosters. Can humans do anything similar?

Human-powered flight has fascinated inventors for decades. And some have even achieved it. In 1979 Bryan Allen piloted the Gossamer Albatross across the English Channel. This 70-pound (32-kilogram) pedal-powered plane made the 22.5-mile (36-km) flight in 2 hours and 49 minutes. To stay up, Allen pedaled nonstop.

Hang gliders rely on rising pockets of air to stay airborne.

More commonly, people achieve unpowered flight with hang gliders. These triangular airfoils produce lift with a running takeoff from a hill or mountain. The glider then catches ridge and thermal lifts to gain **altitude**. Ridge lifts occur when air pushes upward as wind hits a cliff. Thermal lifts are rising hot air pockets. Hang gliders can stay aloft for hours at a time, soaring hundreds of miles.

Wingsuiters may come the closest to feeling like Superman in flight. These daredevils jump from planes wearing suits with arm and leg flaps. The flaps catch air to allow wingsuiters to slow down and glide. While a skydiver reaches 120 miles (193 km) per hour in free fall, wingsuiters fall at only 50 to 60 miles (80 to 97 km) per hour. Slight body movements help wingsuiters steer and change direction in mid-flight. They release parachutes for safe landings.

wingsuit

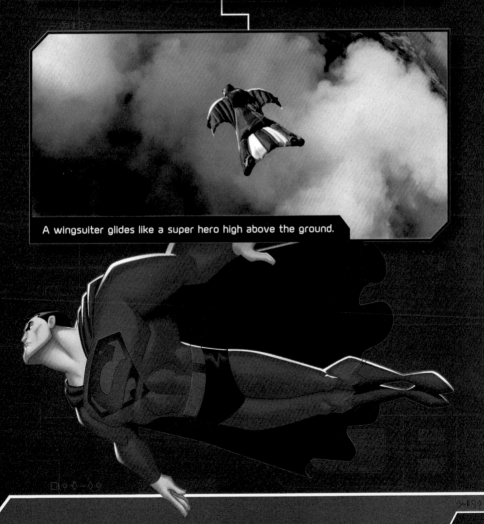

A wingsuiter glides like a super hero high above the ground.

altitude—the height of something above sea level or Earth's surface

JET PACKS

Unpowered flight can only take humans so far. To really fly like Superman, scientists and engineers have stepped up the game with jet packs.

Military engineers began developing jet packs as early as the 1940s. By 1960, Bell Aerosystems produced the Bell Rocket Belt for the U.S. Army. Fueled by hydrogen peroxide, it could stay aloft for only 21 seconds. Although engineers tried changing it to jet power, the military eventually shelved their jet pack plans.

A Bell Rocket Belt 2 is on display at the National Air and Space Museum's Steven F. Udvar-Hazy Center in Chantilly, Virginia.

Riders race above the waves with water-propelled jet packs.

More recently private tinkerers have taken up the quest for functional jet packs. In the early 2000s, Canadian Raymond Li developed a jet pack propelled by water. His Jetlev-Flyer produces up to 500 pounds (227 kg) of thrust to send riders soaring above the water.

Even more amazing are the flying feats of Swiss pilot Yves "Jetman" Rossy. He is famous for flying like an eagle by strapping on a rigid wing with four tiny jet engines. His 15-minute trips reach speeds of up to 190 miles (306 km) per hour. His wings have taken him over the Alps and across the English Channel.

SPRINGTAIL EFV

Jetman Rossy may soon have to share his jet pack fame. The Springtail Exoskeleton Flying Vehicle (EFV) uses a single engine to power fan blades. This futuristic-looking craft can fly for two hours and reach a top speed of 113 miles (182 km) per hour. It can also hover in place.

ALIENS AMONG US

Thrusting his arm skyward, Superman glides between skyscrapers, zooms across the globe, and hovers at will. Obviously, he's not bound by our planet's laws of physics. But are there Earth dwellers among us that also appear to defy natural laws? You bet. Some animals perform unbelievable feats of flight.

ECCENTRIC ANIMALS

You'll find birds, bugs, and Superman hanging out in the sky. But fish, squirrels, and snakes stick to water and land, right? Not all of them. Some amazing critters break beyond their natural habitats.

Imagine cruising the ocean only to see a flying fish soar past at 37 miles (60 km) per hour. Forty species of flying fish live in Earth's oceans. Their rapidly beating tails launch them from the sea to avoid predators. Using wing-like fins, they glide 4 feet (1.2 m) above the water for up to 655 feet (200 m) at a time. That's more than the length of two football fields!

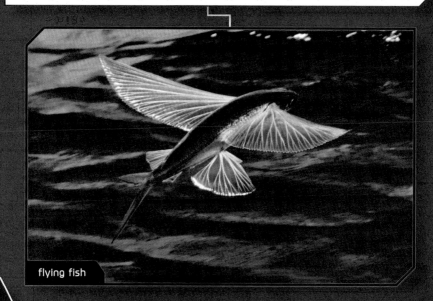

flying fish

Not to be outdone by ocean dwellers, a few unlikely land animals also take to the air. Flying squirrels use flaps between their front and back legs to soar up to 150 feet (46 m) from tree to tree. Paradise tree snakes glide for up to 330 feet (100 m) by flexing their bodies to sail through treetops. And Wallace's flying frogs glide through the jungles of Malaysia and Borneo. How? With **membranes** between their toes and skin flaps on their sides.

flying squirrel

paradise
tree snake

Wallace's flying frog

membrane—thin, flexible layer of tissue or skin

UNBELIEVABLE BIRDS

Flying to the other side of the world is a snap for Superman. In the real world, several bird species make comparable **migrations**. The Arctic tern travels from Greenland to Antarctica each year. This 44,000-mile (71,000-km) trip zigzags across the Atlantic following favorable wind currents. Over its 30-year life span, the tern flies about 1.5 million miles (2.4 million km). That's like flying to the Moon and back three times.

Arctic tern

sooty terns

The Arctic tern flies far, but the tropical sooty tern flies long. It stays airborne from the time it leaves the nest until it returns to lay eggs. Just how long is that? Up to five years! In flight, the sooty tern swoops down to pluck fish from water or to pick-off flying fish. And its shrill call sounds like "wide-a-wake." That's an apt call, since they sleep only a couple of seconds at a time in flight.

HUMMINGBIRD ACROBATICS

The ruby-throated hummingbird can't walk and can barely hop with its tiny legs. But it beats its wings 53 times each second to hover and fly upside down and backward. It also eats twice its weight in food each day to have enough energy to accomplish these feats.

migration—the regular movement of animals as they search different places for food

AMAZING ARTHROPODS

Superman's flight powers are unexplainable. How does he take off unassisted? What keeps him in the air? But sometimes insect flight is equally mystifying.

Insect flight doesn't always follow the same rules as bird and plane flight. Tiny bumblebee wings don't look like airfoils. And they hardly look large enough to keep the husky bees aloft. But by fluttering incredibly fast, bumblebee wings create tiny vortexes. These low-pressure areas above the wings generate lift to keep the bee flying.

bumblebee

FACT:

The painted lady butterfly makes a 4,000-mile (6,437-km) migration from North Africa to Iceland.

blowfly

The blowfly's flight is only understandable with the aid of high-powered X-ray technology. With this technology, scientists discovered the fly uses muscles smaller than human hair to beat its wings 150 times per second. These muscles are not attached directly to its wings. Instead they are inside the fly's **thorax**. As the fly changes the shape of its thorax, the movements are transferred to the wings.

ROBOBEE

Harvard scientists applied their knowledge of a fly's biology to create RoboBee. This tiny robot flaps its paper-thin wings 120 times per second. Future jobs for RoboBee could include crop pollination and search and rescue missions.

thorax—the middle section of an insect's body; wings and legs are attached to the thorax

WONDERS IN MODERN FLIGHT

Seeing the Man of Steel in flight naturally inspires us to want to fly higher and faster. But flight inventions have already achieved some amazing feats—and they're poised to go even higher.

INNOVATION IN FLIGHT

One secret to Superman's success is his ability to outsmart super-villains. Likewise, some of our greatest innovations in flight come from our need to outthink our enemies. It's no wonder the military is such a hotbed for flight innovation.

Spy and stealth planes are military specialties. The SR-71 Blackbird spy plane was one of the fastest planes ever built. It could fly more than 2,000 miles (3,219 km) per hour. That's three times faster than the speed of sound. The aircraft was so fast, it was never hit by a missile in its 25 years of service.

SR-71 Blackbird

Speed is good for making fast getaways. But what about sneaking up on an enemy? That's when you'll need the B-2 Spirit bomber. This 172-foot (52-m) wide boomerang-shaped bomber is virtually undetectable. Its flat black shape and muffled engines keep it hidden in plain sight. More importantly, its composite skin and **radar**-absorbing paint make it look like an insect on radar scanners.

B-2 Spirit

JUMP JETS

Normal fighter jets need long runways for takeoffs and landings. But not the Harrier Jump Jet. It can take off like a helicopter and fly like a jet. Its revolving jet nozzles give it thrust to lift off short runways and small aircraft carriers. Harriers reach speeds of up to 730 miles (1,175 km) per hour in flight.

radar—a device that uses radio waves to track the location of objects

CARGO CARRYING

Between his strength and his ability to fly, Superman makes his job look easy. After all, he can guide crashing passenger jets to the ground without breaking much of a sweat. In the real world, however, lifting cargo takes a huge effort—and a huge plane.

The largest cargo carrier in the world is the Russian Antonov An-225. From front to back and wing tip to wing tip, this beast is nearly the size of a football field. It can carry more than 500,000 pounds (226,800 kg), or the weight of about 50 elephants. It hauls anything up to 33 feet (10 m) in diameter and 230 feet (70 m) long. Loads that can't fit inside it can be carried on the An-225's back. All loaded up, it can still fly 500 miles (800 km) per hour.

The nose of the An-225 flips up so large cargo can be easily loaded.

Super Guppy

NASA's Super Guppy is another huge cargo carrier. The Guppy looks more like a fish than a plane. Its hinged nose opens to reveal a huge cargo bay. It can carry more than 50,000 pounds (23,680 kg) of cargo. Since 1962, this monster has played a vital role in the transportation of spacecraft parts.

TRANSPORT HELICOPTERS

Planes aren't the only heavy lifters. The Mi26 transport helicopter can easily hoist and carry a 737 jetliner. This massive chopper uses an eight-blade propeller. It can carry 20-ton (18-metric ton) loads at 183 miles (295 km) per hour.

DRONES

When super-villains strike, the citizens of Metropolis can count on Superman to swoop in and save the day. In our world, we've discovered ways to sit back and let high fliers handle our toughest jobs. More unmanned aerial vehicles (UAVs) fly our skies today than at any other time in history.

Military UAVs are invaluable in sticky situations. Piloted by a crew miles away, Reaper and Predator drones scout sites ahead of troops or manned vehicles. Pilots use onboard cameras to guide their flights. In the dark, infrared cameras give them night vision. Reapers and Predators help troops in battle by locating and destroying specific targets.

A Predator drone is controlled remotely by a pilot on the ground.

Recreational drones have built-in digital cameras to provide an eye in the sky.

Although military drones have been at work for years, drone use by regular people is rising quickly. Some experts think more than 30,000 drones will be flying overhead in the U.S. alone by 2020. Many owners use their personal drones for making movies and taking photos. And companies are gearing up for drone use too. Agricultural companies have developed drones to help farmers scout crop conditions on large farms. Real estate agents use drones to film virtual tours of houses for sale. One company in England has even tested out drones for pizza delivery.

THE FIRST UAV

UAVs have been around since the 1860s. Charles Perley's aerial bomber was used in the American Civil War (1861–1865). This UAV was a hot air balloon loaded with explosives and a timing mechanism.

INCREDIBLE SPACECRAFT

Superman can fly well beyond the upper reaches of the clouds. Whether guiding a nuclear warhead into space or flying to an alien planet, nothing holds him back. For humans, space flight was only a long-held dream for thousands of years. But now science and engineering give us the power to achieve those dreams.

For more than 50 years, rockets have been our ticket off Earth. They have delivered people to the Moon, robots to Mars, and probes to the very edges of our solar system. While they come in many shapes and sizes, they all work in similar ways. Rockets burn fuel to produce hot gases. These gases expand and blast downward to generate incredible thrust. To escape Earth's gravity, a rocket must reach a speed of 25,000 miles (40,230 km) per hour.

Hot gases burst from the bottom of a rocket to thrust it skyward.

Interstellar—between stars; most often used to describe travel from one star to another

Traveling beyond our solar system is the next space hurdle. But that quest has already begun. In 1977, NASA launched the *Voyager 1* space probe. In 2012, it achieved **interstellar** flight when it reached the edge of our solar system. At its current speed, it would reach our nearest neighboring star in 40,000 years. Unfortunately, *Voyager 1* is expected to run out of fuel around 2025, long before it ever gets there.

An artist's rendition of *Voyager 1* flying through space.

CONCLUSION

No human invention can compete with Superman's command of the skies. He can fly nearly anywhere in the blink of an eye and land with hardly a hair out of place. While we are awed by his grace, science and engineering can still give us a taste of his abilities. From robot bees and massive cargo jets to wingsuits and hang gliders, the science of flight helps us soar.

GLOSSARY

airfoil (AYR-foyl)—a curved surface causing lift in flight

air resistance (AIR ri-ZISS-tuhnss)—the force of air rubbing against things

altitude (AL-ti-tood)—the height of something above sea level or Earth's surface

interstellar (in-tur-STEL-ur)—between stars; most often used to describe travel from one star to another

lift (LIFT)—the upward force of air that causes an object to fly

membrane (MEM-brayn)—thin, flexible layer of tissue or skin

migration (mye-GRAY-shuhn)—the regular movement of animals as they search different places for food

radar (RAY-dar)—a device that uses radio waves to track the location of objects

thermal (THUR-muhl)—having to do with heat or holding in heat

thorax (THOR-aks)—the middle section of an insect's body; wings and legs are attached to the thorax

thrust (THRUHST)—the force that pushes a vehicle forward

READ MORE

Enz, Tammy. *Batplanes and Batcopters: The Engineering Behind Batman's Wings*. Batman Science. North Mankato, Minn.: Capstone, 2014.

Grove, Tim. *Milestones of Flight: From Hot-air Balloons to SpaceShipOne*. New York: Abrams Books for Young Readers, 2016.

Lunis, Natalie. *Gravity-Defying Animals*. Animals with Super Powers. New York: Bearport Publishing, 2014.

Oxlade, Chris. *Stickmen's Guide to Aircraft*. Stickmen's Guides to How Everything Works. Minneapolis: Hungry Tomato, 2016.

INTERNET SITES

FactHound offers a safe, fun way to find Internet sites related to this book. All of the sites on FactHound have been researched by our staff.

Here's all you do:
Visit *www.facthound.com*

Type in this code: 9781515709138

INDEX